Chauncey

and the
Chickens

Give Change a Chance

JULIANNE J. JOHNSON

WestBow Press books may be ordered through booksellers or by contacting:

WestBow Press
A Division of Thomas Nelson & Zondervan
1663 Liberty Drive
Bloomington, IN 47403
www.westbowpress.com
844-714-3454

Illustration by James Yano and Edgardo Silva

ISBN: 978-1-6642-7979-7 (sc)
ISBN: 978-1-6642-7978-0 (e)

Library of Congress Control Number: 2022918262

Print information available on the last page.

WestBow Press rev. date: 10/07/2022

WESTBOW
PRESS®
A DIVISION OF THOMAS NELSON
& ZONDERVAN

For Alex, who flapped and crowed
until I put this story on paper
and for Esmé, whose story this is.

Chauncey is a little girl who lives in a brown brick house at the top of a hill. She has a large flock of laying hens that live in a spacious yet cozy chicken house near the garden. One of Chauncey's chores is to gather the multicolored eggs, a full basket each day.

One day, when she rolled out of her feather bed, she realized that she was very unhappy. "I'm bored with my life," she grumbled. "I'm tired of brushing my teeth, braiding my hair and gathering eggs for breakfast every morning. I'm bored with my toys and riding my bike. I'm lonely on my tire swing. I need a change. I need a vacation…"

Chauncey brushed a feather off her nose and one from her hair and exclaimed, "That gives me a great idea!" Chauncey pulled on her T-shirt, jeans and boots and declared, "I'm going to move out of my room. I'm going to live with the chickens!"

Well, it just so happens that very morning, in the coop on the side of the hill, Rusty the big red rooster cleared his throat and crowed his loudest. "Sun's up! Time to start the day, ladies! Let the egg laying begin!" Three of the hens Opal, Pearl and Jade grumbled in unison, "We're tired of laying eggs for Chauncey's breakfast. We're bored with scratching for bugs and worms in the garden. We need a change! We want a vacation!"

Just then, Chauncey flung open the chicken coop door and crowed her loudest, "Move over, girls, I'm coming in!" As fast as a wink, the trio of unhappy hens saw their chance to break for freedom. They hit the grass and scattered, running as fast as their little chicken feet would carry them to the house on the hill, straight to the porch and through the open screen door.

"This is the life!" they squawked. "Chauncey can have the coop and all the bugs she wants!" The ladies bustled to the pantry in search of a bag of grits. They flew to the top of the piano and while Opal danced on those ivory keys they clucked a merry tune. Every melody they had heard from Chauncey's morning time routine was played, including a jaunty Bach number.

Next up, screen time and Pearl grabbed the remote. The threesome settled onto the plump sofa for a series on backyard poultry farming. Maybe they could see what they were missing out on, why they were so unfulfilled in their own personal poultry palace.

Meanwhile, Chauncey had made herself at home in the coop. The little side door that opened onto the grassy hill and garden looked very inviting, if she could just make the squeeze through the opening to come and go as she pleased. The nesting boxes were a perfect place to stash the contents of her pockets: coins, rocks, gum and a rubber band. Chauncey settled in.

Back at the house, the hens were suddenly feeling cooped up, bored with the bag of grits and channel surfing. They tried to scratch for something, anything in the grooves of the braided rug. They found nothing worth pecking there. A dust bath was virtually impossible in the porcelain tub as well as in the kitchen sink. The windows were locked, there was no possible way to fly out to the grassy yard and hear the chirping birds and feel the wind in their feathers.

11

They began to grumble and complain. It was almost lunchtime. They missed their scratch grains and juicy worms. "It's stuffy in here!" Opal observed. "These grits are tasteless," Pearl chirped. "I've had enough of this," Jade remarked.

Back in the coop, Chauncey had complaints of her own. She began to wish she'd had a bite of breakfast before settling into her new surroundings. Just then, she pushed open the door and spied the hens scurrying back towards her, rushing to return to their home.

They bounced into the little coop lickety-split. "Back so soon?" Chauncey greeted them heartily. "Do you mind if I grab some eggs before I leave? I'm feeling pretty hungry for my breakfast," Chauncey admitted.

"Help yourself," Pearl offered graciously, happy to be back in her familiar surroundings. "There will be plenty more shortly!"

Chauncey hurried to the kitchen and set out all she needed for a Breggies Scramble, her specialty.

As she savored her buttery cubed bread and egg combo, Chauncey hatched another idea.

The hens are so quick to find worms in the garden...
"That gives me a great idea!"

ANNOUNCING: CHAUNCEY'S BAIT SHOP

THE END

CHAUNCEY'S BREGGIES BREAKFAST SCRAMBLE

2 tablespoons butter
6 eggs, beaten
1/2 cup whole milk
2 or 3 slices bread, cubed
Salt and pepper, to taste
Shredded cheese to melt over top

In a large skillet, melt butter. Whisk eggs and milk together. Stir in bread chunks. Add salt and pepper. Pour mixture into melted butter in pan. Cook over medium low heat until fluffy and set. Sprinkle cheese over top and allow to melt. Serve immediately.

Printed in the United States
by Baker & Taylor Publisher Services